BENTHALL HALL

Shropshire

National Trust

Acknowledgements

This guide depends heavily on the previous edition, for which Sir Paul Benthall wrote the text and Mr James Benthall revised the gardens section. The National Trust is grateful to Mr Richard Benthall and Emily Knight for updating the text.

Objects marked with an asterisk (pp.10 [three items], 15) were accepted in lieu of Inheritance Tax by H.M. Government and allocated to the National Trust, 1993.

If you would like to become a member or make a donation, please telephone 0344 800 1895 (minicom 0344 800 4410); write to National Trust, PO Box 574, Manvers, Rotherham S63 3FH; or see our website at: www.nationaltrust.org.uk

Photographs: The Geological Society of London p.18; National Trust Images: Matthew Antrobus pp.6, 19, 20 (top), 22, 23, 31, John Blake p.21, Brian and Nina Chapple front cover, p.20 (bottom), John Hammond pp.1, 4, 5, 12, 15 (top), 25, 26, 27, 28 (top and bottom left and right), 29 (© the artist's estate), 30 (courtesy The Bridgeman Art Library), back cover, Tim Imrie pp.8, 9, 10–11, 13 (top and bottom), 14, 15 (bottom), 16.

Typeset from disc and designed by James Shurmer

Printed by ESP Colour Ltd, Swindon for National Trust (Enterprises) Ltd, Heelis, Kemble Drive, Swindon, Wilts SN2 2NA.
Printed on Novatech Matt FSC Certified paper.

(*Front cover*) Benthall Hall viewed across the Rose Garden

(*Title-page*) A close-up view of the firescreen in the Dining Room showing the Benthall arms

(*Back cover*) Part of the overmantel in the Drawing Room

CONTENTS

THE HOME OF THE BENTHALLS

Benthall Hall has a fascinating history that stretches from medieval times through the Civil War, when it was used as a garrison for Parliamentary troops, and the Industrial Revolution. The present house was the home of the Benthall family from its construction in the late 16th century until 1843 when the estate was sold, but it was never one of those elaborately landscaped estates to which the English gentry retired from the scenes of money-making. No doubt the house, with its fine interior carving and plasterwork, owes its existence chiefly to past owners' profits from mining minerals as well as from farming. Several interesting tenants also made changes to the house and grounds during the 19th century.

Having been brought back into the ownership of the Benthall family in 1934, Benthall Hall is today a welcoming family home. Although none of the contents of the house has been here continuously, one or two of the original pieces have now returned after an absence of more than a century.

Benthall Hall stands in an impressive setting, high above the River Severn, less than a mile to the south-west of the deep rift known as the Severn Gorge. To the east and north the wooded slopes at the edge of the plateau fall precipitously into the valley below, cutting off access from those directions by all wheeled traffic. In consequence, although the industries of Broseley and Coalbrookdale are not far away to the east, and a huge power station has been built only a mile to the north, a rural peace still surrounds the place.

The Shropshire coalfield begins here and runs to the east. For 700 years at least, coal, fireclay and limestone have been mined at Benthall, and the traces of old pits and quarries may be found in many places. Nature, however, soon covered these scars with vegetation, and in due time they became no more than features in the landscape.

At nearby Coalbrookdale, a birthplace of the Industrial Revolution, the smelting of iron with coke began with Abraham Darby in the 18th century and for upwards of a hundred years the area around the Severn Gorge was one of the busiest and most prosperous spots in Britain. Later, decay set in as the industries moved away, and by 1840 the area was in a depressed condition. Revival and repopulation began during the Second World War, and with the coming of Telford New Town in the 1970s another period of industrial expansion began to the east of the Severn.

William and Mary Anne Benthall bought three sets of this 'Flora' pattern (made about 1820 by Rogers of Staffordshire) to cater for their twenty children

(Right) Benthall Hall from the south-west by John Hornby Maw, 1870. The artist was the father of George Maw, a tenant of Benthall Hall in the late 19th century

TOUR OF THE HOUSE

The Exterior

Benthall Hall was originally approached from the south-east via the Chestnut Avenue that can still be seen almost parallel to the lane by which the house is now reached. The change of approach was made in the 18th century.

The house as we see it today is a good example of the domestic architecture of the late 16th century. According to family tradition, it was built in about 1535 and then substantially improved in 1580–5. This does not accord with the general style of the architecture, which suggests construction about 1580. However, during the re-roofing of the north wing in 1998, it was discovered that the earliest part of that wing is timber-framed in the style of 1500–30 and that the timber framing was later covered

with a brick skin. Various additions and changes were made in the house from time to time, but during the 20th century these have mostly been removed. The exterior is now nearly as it appeared at the end of the 16th century. In fact, the south and west fronts are almost intact.

The walls are built mostly of sandstone taken from a nearby quarry. The asymmetrical front, with its mullioned and transomed windows, has a charm which depends chiefly on an unusual feature: a pair of five-faced bay windows which rise through two storeys and are surmounted by low parapets below the level of the windows in the top storey. At the western end there is a rectangular projection forming large rooms within, and on the west front there is a third tier

The south front

of bay windows similar to those on the south front. The five gables that break the roofline and the four 16th-century chimneystacks in moulded brick contribute to the harmony of the composition.

The Entrance Porch shows signs of having been added after the wall behind it was built and, as it contains a hiding place, may well have been added soon after 1583 to shelter Catholic priests fleeing religious persecution. The front door on the west wall of the porch has a low opening with a round arch. In Victorian times it was blocked up and a taller doorway was opened in the south wall in place of the window. The original arrangement was restored in 1964.

Above the door on the west wall are five stone tablets in a quincunx (arranged like a five in a pack of cards). The same pattern occurs again in tablets in the south wall of the porch, although the left-hand upper tablet is missing. The marks are thought to allude to the five wounds of Christ, representations of which formed the banner of the so-called Pilgrimage of Grace in 1536–7, the first rebellion in England by Catholics against Henry VIII. The marks may have been meant to indicate to strangers that the house was owned by Catholic sympathisers, and that priests might expect help within. It has been suggested that the words 'Five for the symbols at your door' in the old song 'Green grow the rushes O' refer to this practice. As the other words in the song have religious associations, the phrase would at least seem to indicate that five symbols at a door have a religious meaning.

Curiously enough a hiding place exists directly inside the two sets of marks, though this was probably meant to conceal valuables or religious articles rather than people. One of the tablets on the west side above the door bears the date 1535, but this has clearly been added in fairly recent times. The centre tablet on the south front bears the initials BLK, which stand for the Lawrence Benthall who owned the house from 1623 to 1652 and his wife Katherine. No doubt these were added to replace an earlier mark long after the porch was built. Marks in the same pattern are prominent at Boscobel House,

which was built as a training centre for priests and contains many secret chambers and other such devices; they also occur a few miles from Benthall at Madeley Court, where several hiding places are known to have existed.

The Interior

THE ENTRANCE HALL

The Porch leads into the Entrance Hall and there is evidence that there was a further external door on the opposite north wall, which was later blocked. It is likely that there would have been a screens passage at the eastern end linking these two doorways and separating the Hall from the Kitchen and associated quarters; the fireplace would then have been centrally positioned on the north wall.

The floor was originally stone-flagged, probably with the same type of stone used for the two sets of rounded steps at the western end of the Hall. These steps could be all that remains of the raised platform or dais at the 'high' end of the Hall, furthest away from the screen. The flagstones were replaced in 1859 with locally made tiles with designs inspired by medieval heraldic patterns. These were manufactured by Maw & Co. of Jackfield when the house was occupied by the brothers George and Arthur Maw, who ran the tile works and were tenants of Lord Forester's Willey estate. Although the tiles seem to be standard Maw patterns, the design of the floor is very individual and colourful, and was probably designed by George Maw himself. The tiles were covered by the present oak floor in 1918.

Most of the other woodwork dates from the 18th century, when the room was damaged by fire. The overmantel, made about 1630, survived the fire and displays the arms of Benthall impaled with Cassy and Giffard. Lawrence Benthall (d.1652) married Katherine Cassy of Whitfield, Gloucestershire, whose mother was a Giffard of Chillington, Staffordshire, the family that built Boscobel House and owned it in the 17th century.

Benthall, *or a lion rampant double queued azure ducally crowned gules;*
Crest, *on a coronet or a leopard statant argent spotted sable;*
Cassy, *argent a chevron between three wyverns' heads erased;*
Giffard, *azure three stirrups with leathers or.*

The shield seems to be heraldically incorrect, but it makes a clear statement of rank.

It is believed that the oak refectory table was made for the room about 1640, though it was absent for many years, returning only in 1963. At the eastern end of the big table is a heavy chair made of turned ash, which by tradition was the chair of the abbot of Neath Abbey near Swansea. It cannot be dated with any degree of certainty because chairs of this type were made in England for centuries. The oak armchair at the other end of the table dates from about 1600.

The large oak cupboard at the west end of the room dates from about the first half of the 17th century. The cabinet with tortoise-shell inlays is Flemish work of the 17th century but it was much altered in the 19th century.

The dresser is a 17th-century Welsh mule chest with a hinged top. The hinge arrangement was altered in the 18th century when the top was added to display pewter or pottery. The pewter in the room is Welsh and, as is customary in Wales, has been polished on the

(Left) The Entrance Hall

(Right) The armour in the Entrance Hall is made up from more than one suit

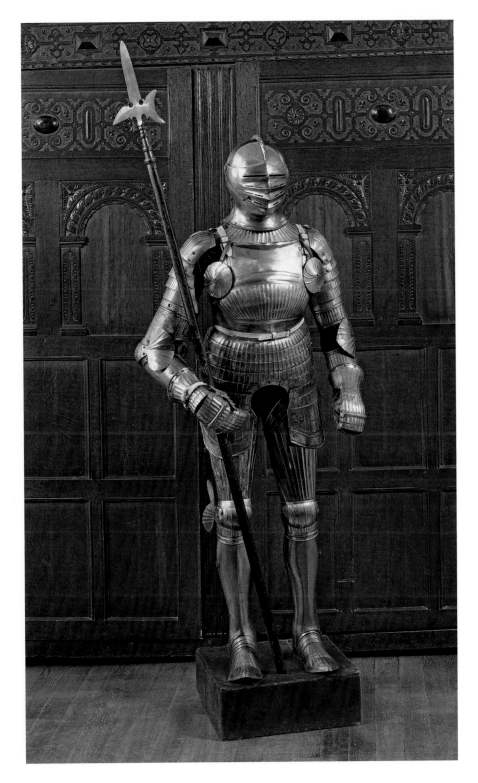

back. Pewter plates were bought in sets of 36 called a 'garnish' and paid for by the pound.

The suit of armour partly dates from the 16th century, but has been repaired at a later date. Its helmet was made in Nuremberg about 1525, but does not belong to the rest of the suit, which is mostly of rather earlier date.

THE DINING ROOM

The warm tones of the 17th-century oak panelling in this room were for a time covered with white paint, but this was removed in 1935. The original decorated plaster ceiling remained until the middle of the 19th century; a surviving fragment, part of a roundel depicting a goat, is displayed in the porch.

Lawrence Benthall added the arms of Benthall impaled with Cassy to the overmantel in about 1630. The fireplace was added later, having been designed in 1756 by Thomas Farnolls Pritchard, the Shrewsbury architect who was partly responsible for the design of the iron bridge at Coalbrookdale. The fossil-rich crinoid marble would probably have come from a quarry in Yorkshire.

The oak dining-table dates from about 1625, as do the two chairs with acorns, which are north-country or Scottish. The other two pairs of chairs at the table are early 18th-century, the taller pair having the date 1729 carved on the back. The livery cupboard is Elizabethan.

The armorial porcelain in this room was made in China at various dates in the late 18th century, possibly for Thornton Benthall, who was a ship's purser with the East India Company. It shows the arms of Benthall quartered with those of Wolrich and Dudmaston. The marriage with a Shropshire heiress commemorated by these quarterings took place in the 14th century, more than 400 years before the porcelain was made.

The Caughley (pronounced 'calf-ley') porcelain* exhibited here, in the Drawing Room and in the Library, was manufactured about two miles away in the period 1775 to 1800. These items were collected by Sir Paul and Lady Benthall and were given to the National Trust by their family on Sir Paul's death in 1992.

The Dining Room

(Left) The Chinese porcelain in the Dining Room was bought by Thornton Benthall, whose statuette is on the same shelf

(Right, top) The Drawing Room

(Right, bottom) The small statuette of an old lady on top of the chest-of-drawers in the Drawing Room is made of beeswax and dates from around 1620

THE DRAWING ROOM

The Drawing Room is fully panelled and has a magnificent plaster ceiling. A number of repairs and alterations have taken place since the panelling was installed in about 1630. One theory to explain the ill-fitting corners is that the room originally extended to the north wall of the house and included the western bay window but, perhaps because of the difficulty in warming such a large room with so many windows, the panelling on the north wall was moved inwards to reduce the size of the room. A more likely theory is that the panelling was made mostly for some other room or house and was fitted into this room by Lawrence Benthall, who then engaged craftsmen to make the overmantel, including the coat of arms of his wife and himself.

Some of the original oak panelling has been replaced by inferior wood, probably after damage caused by Civil War fighting in 1645 (see page 26). As a result, the woodwork has been covered with paint for many years, the present off-white colour having been applied in 1960.

The elaborate ceiling and frieze, the work of Italian craftsmen, were added after the panelling was installed. Each of the six ceiling panels has a different strap work design, the common factor being the central oval bosses. The ceiling was described in 1929 by H. Avray Tipping in his book *English Homes*:

Above the wainscoting the plasterer was employed to emulate the joiner. Strap-work and jewelling fill the ceiling panels, while the frieze shows more ambitious treatment. There are roundels wrought with a variety of beasts (such as the lion, the griffin, the horse, and the stag), and between them birds hold one end of the drapery that forms part of the scroll work.

A man's head is also visible on the north wall.

The fireplace, in common with the one in the Dining Room, was designed by Thomas Farnolls Pritchard in 1756. Designs for both fireplaces are in an album of his drawings now in the Library of the American Institute of Architects in Washington DC.

Despite its oriental appearance, the lacquer cabinet is English, made in London about 1670. The walnut tallboy dates from 1710 and the walnut cabinet with two doors about 1690. The oak chest-of-drawers inlaid with mother-of-pearl and other materials was made about 1650. There is a similar chest in the Victoria and Albert Museum bearing the date 1653 and another may

be seen at Montacute House in Somerset (also in the care of the National Trust).

THE STAIRCASE

The staircase is the best feature of the house. Of cantilever construction, it is believed to have been built in 1618. The lower sections show evidence of having been lowered by five or six inches at some stage. The massive newel posts at the corners of the balustrade are carved with grotesque heads, and the leopard of the Benthall crest occupies a panel at the turn of the stairs, while a flight higher a similar panel contains the double-tailed lion from the coat of arms. In addition, wyverns from the Cassy arms are carved in the panels below the balustrading. The top nine inches or so of the newel posts were possibly added much later, probably in Victorian times. The treads were renewed after 1818, when a fire broke out near the top of the main staircase during the night. A servant galloped to the village to summon help and, with the help of the

13

The Staircase seen from the first floor landing

(Right) The Etruscan funerary urn at the foot of the staircase was discovered by the engineer Thomas Brassey while he was excavating for a railway in Tuscany

'Lady in a Persian Dress' by F.R.Pickersgill (Staircase)
The woman in the painting was the artist's wife and great-
grandmother of the Hon. Lady Ruth Benthall

villagers, formed a bucket chain and put out the fire but not before much damage had been done.

It is possible that the original staircase, prior to 1618, occupied the small rooms on each floor situated immediately behind the present staircase. The space now occupied by the stairs at ground level could have been a parlour or private chamber when the house was built.

The doorcases and plasterwork are of the 1840s. Similar work survives in the Valley Hotel, Ironbridge, which was formerly a private house and was occupied for a while in the second half of the 18th century by Alfred Maw. At the foot of the stairs is an alabaster funerary urn from Etruria in Italy that dates from about 200 BC. The figure is an effigy of the deceased and the scene on the front portrays the journey through the underworld. The pottery displayed on the staircase is by Rogers of Staffordshire, made about 1820 in the 'Flora' design. William Searle Benthall (d.1854) and his wife Mary Anne purchased three full sets of this crockery to cater for their twenty children.

THE GREAT CHAMBER OR LIBRARY

For many years this large room directly above the Hall was divided into two bedrooms and a passage but it was restored to its original state in 1960. An indication of the placement of the partition walls is given by the position of the 17th-century panelling to the right of the fireplace and towards the south end of the east and west walls.

The large bookcase at the west end of the room dates from about 1740. At the east end is a late 18th-century cabinet containing black pottery of the same period. Some of the best pieces were made in Staffordshire but many are from local potteries at Jackfield near Broseley.

The oak cradle for twin babies is early 17th century in style but bears the date 1680, when it was presumably given to the two children whose names, Elizabeth and John, are inscribed on one end.

All the portraits and most of the portrait miniatures* in this room are of the Benthall family.

15

THE WEST BEDROOM

This is the master bedroom for Edward and Sally Benthall. The furniture includes the English mahogany tallboy dated to around 1800, and two teak cabinets made in Calcutta for Sir Paul and Lady Benthall in the 1930s by cabinet makers Guha & Sons and painted white.

There are a number of watercolours painted by Annie Theodosia Benthall, the wife of the Rev. Charles Benthall displayed in the room.

THE PORCH ROOM

An interesting old door on the far side of the Library leads to a small room over the porch. It has been referred to as the Priest's Room but there is no evidence to suggest that a priest was housed here or that the room was used as a chapel. Beneath its floor is a hiding place that was rediscovered in 1935 after having been forgotten for many years.

The room now contains some old prints and other items connected with Boscobel House, including an oak carving depicting the escape of Charles II from Boscobel after the Battle of Worcester. The small tree at the bottom refers to the story of his hiding in an oak to evade Cromwell's troops. The carving was owned by Mary Clementina Benthall, a descendant of one of the Penderel brothers who helped the King to hide at Boscobel. There are also two small 15th-century oil paintings, and furniture dating from the 16th or early 17th century, including a bible box made in about 1680.

THE EAST BEDROOM

Another bedroom used by the family when they stay at Benthall Hall. The furniture includes a black lacquered Queen Anne chest of drawers, around 1710, and a Queen Anne dressing table. The high-backed chair is English Victorian with modern embroidery.

Other miscellaneous items include a Chippendale-style gilt mirror dated to around 1760, and a portrait of a lady in a gilt frame thought to be the Queen of Bohemia, from the circle of Johnson, 17th century.

THE STUDY

This room is now used as a study by the family. Sir Paul Benthall's desk was presented to him on his retirement from India. There are some paintings from India and a number of family portraits on display.

THE LINEN ROOM

Not surprisingly the house's linen is stored here. In the Victorian period it would have made up part of the servants' quarters. During the 20th century, the room was redesigned as a parlour and remains a family sitting room today. The Delft tiles originate from this period and would have been placed around the fireplace, probably by the Maws.

The shields show the coats-of-arms of the families who married into the Benthall family. The exit up the staircase into the East Bedroom is a later 18th-century addition. The wall in which the blocked-up window can be seen, was originally an external wall.

(Left) Most of the panelling in the Great Chamber dates from the 17th century

THE GARDEN AND PARKLAND

HISTORY

There is no record of the appearance of any formal garden before the 18th century, though it seems that the boundaries were roughly the same as today. An open area of grass to the east of the house, flanked by an ancient yew and known as 'the Bowling Green' appears to be the only surviving feature, and this is thought to be Elizabethan.

The documented history of the garden starts with the tenancy of the brothers George and Arthur Maw a little before 1860. As early as

1872 William Robinson, writing in *The Garden,* described the garden and its many plants as 'cultivated with no common skill'. George Maw, a local tile manufacturer, travelled extensively in Europe, Turkey, North Africa and North America and collected many plants. Among them was the plant that has become known in gardens as *Chionodoxa luciliae,* the Glory of the Snow, though it has not been determined botanically.

Maw grew a great quantity of alpine and bulbous plants and among them many species of *Crocus.* Bulbs, presumably of his collection, flower annually at Benthall. Many of the choicer kinds were grown in sunken frames; this is the cause of the lengthy hollow to the south-east of the house (the trees have grown since then). His success with crocuses led him to write a beautifully illustrated book, *The Genus Crocus,* which was completed in 1886. It is still a standard work on the subject and very scarce. Of his naturalised plantings *Crocus speciosus* and *Crocus pulchellus,* both from the Middle East, and *Crocus nudiflorus* from northern Spain and south-west France, still flourish and flower regularly in autumn, but have not hybridised; in the spring there are many *Crocus tommasinianus* from Dalmatia, and *Crocus vernus* from the Alps and the Pyrenees, while *Lilium martagon,* the Turk's Cap Lily, is also naturalised.

The next tenants, Robert Bateman and his wife, lived at Benthall from about 1890 to 1906. Bateman, from a Staffordshire family, was an architect practising in London and Birmingham and was also a painter of some note. His father was James Bateman, the creator of the famous garden at Biddulph Grange (now in the care of

(Left) George Maw's crocus drawings were descibed by John Ruskin as 'most exquisite … and quite beyond criticism'

The dovecote in the Rose Garden was built by Robert Bateman, who lived in the house from about 1890 to 1906. Bateman's parents created the garden at Biddulph Grange in Staffordshire, now also protected by the National Trust

the National Trust). He made some additions and alterations to the church, probably including the girl's head on the west end, and the little statue in the middle of the lily pond. He and his wife laid out the terraces and rockeries. The terraced garden to the west of the house was known as the Pixy Garden in the Batemans' day (now the Rose Garden) and Robert is thought to have built the octagonal dovecote.

THE GARDEN TODAY

In 1962 Sir Paul and Lady Benthall began, with much help and encouragement from the National Trust, to restore the garden from the weedy overgrown state into which it had slipped during the Second World War. The whole garden was much exposed to cold winds from the north and east, and one of their first acts was to create shelter by planting trees beyond and around the old walled kitchen garden, which was laid out before 1843. Trees were also planted to shield the garden from westerly gales and others in an attempt to screen the nearby electricity pylons which were erected during their tenancy.

Some poplars were planted for short-term effect while slower trees are maturing. They also did much other new planting, introducing fruit trees and bulbs.

James Benthall and his wife Jill, who became the tenants in 1985, found the garden once again in a rather neglected state, as Sir Paul's failing eyesight had made it difficult for him to supervise the work. Their first task was to establish a standard of maintenance and care, and to carry out extensive planting where necessary in order to restore colour and interest, including clematis as well as many new shrub and climbing roses. They managed, over a period of about five years, to control some serious infestations of *Petasites fragrans*, the winter heliotrope, and replanted the rockery banks with suitable ground-cover plants, adding to the garden's variety without losing its unique character.

The old kitchen garden presented a problem. There was a herbaceous border and established fruit trees, but the rest was still taken up by large areas of vegetable beds, a soft fruit cage and a hard tennis court. One of their first decisions was to grass in a large part of the vegetable beds.

*(Left) The Walled
Kitchen Garden features
a wide herbaceous
border created by James
and Jill Benthall*

*(Right) The garden is
full of colour during the
summer months*

Soon afterwards they created a herb and dyeplant garden in the remains of the old greenhouse with plants such as madder, woad, dyers' greenweed and false indigo. Jill had a long-standing interest in spinning, weaving and dyeing, and soon also developed an interest in dried flowers.

James and Jill also influenced some of the planting in the kitchen garden. The tall south-facing wall of the kitchen garden had to be partly rebuilt about 1992 and at the same time the dilapidated tennis court was removed. This gave James and Jill the opportunity to plant a collection of crab apples in the form of two linked quincunxes, and to create a new wide border in front of the wall. This becomes very hot in summer, so any planting had to take this into account. Paths were made for easy working, and arches were built to provide carefully sited seating against the wall and, along the main path, to draw the eye away from the intrusive pylons in the field beyond the garden. At this time it was agreed that the area of the garden open to visitors would be extended to include the old Kitchen Garden and also the Wilderness where the crocuses and lilies are naturalised.

View of the west front from the Rose Garden

The emphasis running through the work that James and Jill carried out in the garden was to maintain the existing character of each part, to add variety and interest and to make the garden as trouble-free as possible, although it inevitably remains quite labour-intensive. Richard and Stella Benthall have continued this policy, making changes only where plants have to be replaced or trees have to be removed as they become too large. The property has benefited from a succession of family tenants who have been able to create an attractive plantsman's garden.

THE PARKLAND

A small area of parkland lies to the south of the Hall and round an avenue of horse chestnuts which, approaching the house from the south east, shows where the main drive had been until the present drive was constructed in the late 18th century.

The land, like so much of the old Benthall estate, had been subject to small scale coal-

mining over long periods but, in the 1940s, the whole of the meadow to the west of the chestnut avenue became an open-cast mine. Subsequently refilled and relandscaped, the ground has been repastured and some parkland trees have been planted, creating a fine rural scene between the Hall and the village a mile away.

Immediately to the north of the Hall stood the medieval village of Benthall – apparently razed to the ground in September 1645 when Benthall, having lately fallen to the Parliamentary forces, was besieged by the Royalists. Part of the site has been damaged by ploughing and by surface mining of coal, but that which lies in the old pasture adjacent to the lane is a well-preserved hollow way as well as the earthworks of former house platforms, enclosures and broad ridge-and-furrow cultivation marks. The only vernacular survivors of the original Benthall village, a pair of timber-framed barns belonging to Benthall Farm (in private tenancy) and dating from the early 17th century lie between the earthworks and the Hall.

BENTHALL CHURCH

The present church was built in 1667 and has had no direct connection with the Hall for nearly four hundred years. A church certainly existed before 1221, but Benthall did not become a separate parish until the reign of Elizabeth I. The original church was probably a private chapel for the Hall. All that remains of it is the font, which is possibly Saxon, and some 13th-century decorated tiles in the floor. It is not even certain that the old church was built on the site of the present church, though this is probable.

During the Civil War the church was badly damaged. On its rebuilding in 1667, the dedication was changed from St Brice, an early Welsh missionary, to St Bartholomew. As Celtic churches were often dedicated to their founders, it is possible that the first chapel was founded by St Brice himself. Only one other church in England was dedicated to St Brice – at Brize Norton in Oxfordshire. The festivals of St Brice and St Bartholomew were both known for the terrible massacres that occurred on them; on St Brice's Day, 13 November 1002 for example, King Ethelred ordered a slaughter of the Danes, hence William the Conqueror's battle cry at Hastings: 'Remember St Brice'.

The present porch and apsidal extension at the west end were added in 1893, but the old door with long hinges ending in flame-like ornamentation has survived in a new position. A curious sundial on the south wall was added at the end of the 19th century and restored in 1962. Below it is the stone head of a lion, the mouth of which forms the entrance to a beehive in the gallery of the church, which has often harboured bees.

Hatchments of the Benthall and Browne families hang in the nave, and in the chancel is an interesting monument to the Brownes protected by an iron grille. The pulpit, with its three carved panels, is Jacobean. The new memorial to members of the Benthall family was designed and made by Richard Kindersley.

(Left) 'Out of the strong came forth sweetness': the mouth of the stone lion below the sundial forms the entrance to a beehive in the church gallery

(Right) Benthall church was rebuilt in 1667 after sustaining damage during the Civil War

BENTHALL AND THE BENTHALLS

The name Benthall is derived from Anglo-Saxon words meaning a field overgrown with bent grass. The name has been variously spelt Benethale, Benetala, Benthall, Bentall and in several other ways. Probably most, if not all, the families now called Bentall, Benthall and Benthal took their name from here, but some may have originated from another place of the same name near Ford, to the west of Shrewsbury. The place name is now pronounced to rhyme with 'gentle', but most, if not all, English people bearing the name, however it may be spelt, pronounce it as if they were speaking of a 'bent awl'. In America, where there are many people called Benthall, the 'th' is usually pronounced as in 'thing'.

EARLY HISTORY

The place is recorded in the Domesday Book as part of Wenlock. From the time of Edward the Confessor, and possibly earlier, the estate had belonged to the priory of Wenlock. Members of the family that took its name from the place were described at various times as lords of the manor and would have held the property from the priory. The first well-documented member of the family was Anfrid de Benetala (d. after 1128), who attended a chapter at Castle Holgate, Shropshire, in 1100, attested a charter in 1120, and was probably lord of the manor. Two heralds who visited Shropshire on different occasions in the 16th century are recorded as stating that they had seen deeds or charters in Anglo-Saxon that documented the family's existence here before the Norman Conquest. Unfortunately, as the deeds bore no dates they could not be used to carry the pedigree back before Anfrid. The deeds are believed to have been last in the possession of Francis Benthall (d.1903), a solicitor, and they

have not since been traced. Francis recorded three generations before Anfrid, presumably on the evidence of the deeds, but in 1961 no evidence of the former existence of the deeds could be found in the College of Arms.

It has been suggested that the Hall and Porch of the present house are built on the ground plan of the original Saxon house, and that some of the oak beams which support the roof of the cellars of the Tudor building were originally part of a Saxon house. The presence in Benthall church of a font believed to be of Saxon origin suggests that the original chapel, which certainly existed before 1221, may have dated back to the 11th century. In a dispute with the Prior of Wenlock, Robert de Benethal (d.c.1249) argued that his ancestors had built the chapel in the distant past and had maintained it thereafter. As the chapel was not a parish church until 1590, it seems likely that it was built to serve the dwelling house that certainly existed in 1274 and may have been there before the Norman Conquest.

After Anfrid the succession of the estate is clear. Although many references to the people who lived at Benthall survive from earlier times, the first recorded reference to a house dates from 1250 when Philip de Benthall (d.c.1281) is recorded as granting to Buildwas Abbey the right to carry stone and coal over his land in Benthall Edge, and as giving the Abbey some land lying between Benthall and Buildwas. In 1270 Philip became involved in what appears to have been a feud with a family in Broseley, and it may have been this that eventually resulted in his losing his rights to the estate. In 1274 he complained that his church and house had been plundered by men claiming to be the king's officers.

On his death, Philip left three daughters but no son. In 1283 the estate was acquired by

Robert Burnell, Bishop of Bath and Wells and Lord Chancellor of England. In the same year, a relative of his, John Burnell, married Margery, the youngest daughter of Philip, and obtained from Robert the Benthall estate (which had already been in Margery's family for at least six generations). As a result, no doubt, of his relationship with the powerful chancellor, John was allowed to use a coat of arms incorporating a crowned lion, a modification of the Burnell coat (*Argent a lion rampant sable crowned and armed or*). This coat was the subject of the first recorded plea of arms which took place during the siege of Calais in 1346–7.

From John Burnell the estate passed to his elder son Philip, who is described as Philip Burnell de Benethale in a deed dated 1322 (still in the possession of the family). From him the estate descended in the male line to William Benthall (d.1572), who is believed to have built the present house, or part of it. The name Burnell was dropped after a few generations, though strictly it should have been borne by all descendants of John.

For over 300 years, up to the 16th century, the great events of history passed Benthall by and the inhabitants made no mark outside their immediate neighbourhood. The family history becomes little more than a catalogue of marriages with Shropshire families and of occasional appointments to local offices. The most notable member in this long period was perhaps Henry, the second son of John Burnell, who became Abbot of Buildwas, and remained so until his death in 1317.

No doubt a house existed on or near the present site of Benthall, and in all probability the massive masonry at the east end of the present house was part of the medieval buildings. At the west end of the house, floor tiles made in the 13th century have recently been dug up from where they were thrown, perhaps when the house was rebuilt about 1535 or 1583. In the troubled times of Elizabeth I the family was Catholic in sympathy, if not in practice, and no doubt its members felt the need to shelter priests. The remains of hiding places suggest that they may

have been made by the famous Brother Owen, who spent most of his life contriving hiding places in various parts of England. After the failure of the Gunpowder Plot, he was tortured to death in the Tower of London, successfully resisting all attempts to extort from him information about his life's work.

THE CIVIL WAR

More eventful times came in 1642, when Lawrence Benthall was owner of the estate. He had married Katherine Cassy of Whitfield, Gloucestershire, and had made many improvements to the interior of the house. On the outbreak of the Civil War King Charles I made his headquarters for a time at Shrewsbury, where he rallied many of the local gentry to his cause. Col. Lawrence Benthall fortified his house for the King and, in March 1643, commanded

Detail of the overmantel in the Dining Room. Lawrence Benthall used heraldic decoration to celebrate the union of the Benthall and Cassy families

The oak carving in the Priest's Room shows the escape of Charles II from Boscobel House after the Battle of Worcester. It was brought to the house by Mary Clementina Benthall, a descendant of one of the Penderel brothers who helped the King to hide at Boscobel

the garrison in a successful attack on a Parliamentary plundering party led by Colonel Mytton of Wem. For two years or more the King's garrison at Benthall seems to have been maintained but, in February 1645, the Royalist stronghold of Shrewsbury fell to a surprise night-time attack led by the same Colonel Mytton. The surrounding country soon came under Parliamentary control and in July a Parliamentary garrison occupied Benthall. At this time the neighbourhood of Benthall and Broseley was one of the most important coalfields in the west of England, producing about 30,000 tons of coal a year. The Benthall garrison was valued by the Parliamentary leaders as a base from which to command the River Severn and to prevent its use for carrying coal to the Royalists at Bridgnorth and Worcester and further down-river. Its strategic importance was recognised by the King's men too, and later

in the same year a Royalist force, drawn from the garrisons of Bridgnorth, Worcester and Ludlow, made an attack on Benthall Hall at daybreak. After an hour's hard fighting, during which several of the attackers were killed, the Royalists were forced to withdraw to Bridgnorth. From the damage done to the window and the panelling, it appears that the assault was made on the south window of the Drawing Room.

Extract from Dispatches to Parliament:

…we have planted a Garrison at Benthall to prevent the enemy from gathering contributions in their country, and to stop coles coming thither, and to Worcester, for at this place the coles that supplyed those places are digged. This garrison doth much annoy the enemy, and at our first coming to fortify here the enemy sent forth severall parties from Worcester, Ludlow, and Bridgnorth, who joyned together with intent to frustrate our design here, and to that end made an attempt against us in the night, or about break of day in the morning, but we were so gallantly received, that it is conceived they will not be hastly to come again, for we slew divers of them, and after about an houre's fight forced them to retire to Bridgenorth, from whence they came.

Lawrence and Katherine's son, Cassius Benthall (1623–46), was by then an ensign in the King's army. He had been taken prisoner at the fall of Shrewsbury, but had subsequently escaped and, though not more than 23 years old, was promoted colonel. He was killed in March 1646 at Stow-on-the-Wold where the King's last field army was completely destroyed.

Among those who fought with Cassius was Thomas Penderel, who lived on the estate of the Giffard family near Chillington, some twelve miles east of Benthall. He was taken prisoner at Stow and deported to the West Indies. Five years later, in 1651, King Charles II, escaping after his defeat at Worcester, came as a fugitive to Boscobel House, which the Roman Catholic Giffard family had built near Chillington as a secret seminary for priests. There the King was befriended by the Giffards and by five brothers and a brother-in-law of Thomas Penderel, some of whom were acting as caretakers of Boscobel. Accompanied by Richard Penderel, one of the brothers, Charles set out on foot with the intention of crossing the Severn and escaping to Wales. With blistered feet he reached the village of Madeley, only to hear that all the river crossings, including the ferry near where the iron bridge now stands, were guarded by enemy cavalry. As the hiding place at Madeley Court, on the opposite side of the bridge to Benthall, was generally known he lay hidden in a barn. Charles then eventually returned to Boscobel, where followed his concealment in an oak tree.

It seems that Lawrence Benthall narrowly missed the honour of helping Charles II to escape; where other than Benthall Hall could Richard Penderel have been intending to guide the footsore King beyond the Severn? As a dependant of the Giffards, Richard must have known of the house of their relatives at Benthall, which lay less than a mile beyond the place where he intended to cross the river. When the war was over Lawrence Benthall returned to his home but was heavily fined for his loyalty to the King and had to face the great damage done to his property.

During the Civil War the chapel at Benthall was more or less destroyed, and the outbuildings and the village lying to the north of the house razed to the ground in order to prevent their occupation by the enemy. The village was never rebuilt on the old site but new cottages were erected half a mile to the east nearer to the coal-mines.

THE 18TH AND 19TH CENTURIES

Lawrence was succeeded by his eldest son Philip Benthall, who died in 1713 aged 81 and was buried in the chancel of Benthall church. His successor was his son Richard, who died in 1720, leaving no children, and was also buried there. Richard's uncle, Edward Benthall, had left a daughter, Katherine, who had married Ralph Browne of Caughley Hall, near Broseley. Their children included a daughter named Elizabeth. Before he died, Richard settled his estate on his

Portrait of Abigail Thornton, c. 1690. Abigail was the wife of the Rev. William Thornton of Birkin, Yorkshire, and mother of Elizabeth Bentall (Great Chamber)

Portrait of Elizabeth Bentall, c. 1760–80 (Great Chamber)

From Ralph Browne, Benthall passed to his wife's niece, who married the Rev. Edward Harries, whose son, Francis Blythe Harries, was the owner until 1843. After the 1818 fire, a new wing containing a large dining room was built at the east end of the house. In 1962 this was demolished except for two rooms in the basement, leaving a raised terrace.

In 1844 the house was sold to the 2nd Lord Forester, the owner of the neighbouring Willey estate, and from 1845 to about 1930 Benthall Hall was occupied by various tenants. The most notable was George Maw, FLS, FAS, FGS, the distinguished botanist, who assembled a collection of rare plants in the garden (see p.18).

In about 1860 the house was divided into two dwellings. A staircase was added behind the main staircase and a two-storeyed wing was built on the north-west, but this was demolished in 1935 and only its tiled floor and a stone table mark the site. The second staircase has also now gone.

cousin Elizabeth, a step which resulted on his death in litigation when the estate was claimed by his two sisters. In 1746 the case was decided by the House of Lords in favour of the Brownes and the property passed to another Ralph Browne, the last descendant of the Benthalls to own it for well over a century.

Around 1700 a small pottery stood on the Browne family's Caughley estate near a coal-pit on a plateau high above the Severn. Thomas Turner, who had acquired experience of porcelain manufacture at the factories in Bristol and Worcester, started a porcelain works on the site of the pottery in around 1754. The new factory, despite its isolation and difficult approaches, became a rival to the famous Worcester factory. It was sold to John Rose of Coalport in 1799 but continued to operate until 1814, when the plant was moved to Coalport. A collection of the porcelain made at Caughley between 1775 and 1799 is displayed in the Dining Room, the Drawing Room and the Library.

The silhouettes of Edward and Clementina Benthall were drawn at the time of their marriage in 1842 (Great Chamber)

Meanwhile, the descendants of a younger son of William, the supposed builder of the house in 1535, had settled in Essex, meeting with varied fortunes in various walks of life. In the 19th century two branches of this family had each founded a firm that became well-known public companies bearing the name of Bentall. A third branch had moved from Essex to Devon in the 18th century and prospered there, acquiring property, including the ruins of Buckfast Abbey.

Through the vicissitudes of several centuries this branch maintained an interest in their place of origin in Shropshire. They kept relics of Benthall, including some of the medieval title deeds, made visits there, passing on to their children notes and sketches of what they found, and at one time owned a small property in the neighbourhood. In 1843, when the Benthall estate came up for sale, a member of the Devon branch, Edward Benthall, then a judge in Bengal, tried to buy it. However, in his absence in India he was outbid by Lord Forester.

THE BENTHALLS RETURN

Over 70 years later, in 1918, a son of Edward's, the Rev. Charles Benthall (1861–1936), obtained a lease of the house and lived there for a few years with his family. In 1934 the property again came up for sale and might have been dismantled and shipped to the USA if it had not been bought by Mary Clementina Benthall (1879–1960). Mary Clementina was a granddaughter of Edward Benthall, the Bengal judge, and her husband James Floyer Dale was Edward's grandson. (They then changed their names from Dale to Benthall.) She had a double interest in Benthall, being descended through her mother from John Penderel, one of the five brothers who saved Charles II at Boscobel.

James Floyer Benthall died in 1942 and in 1958 Clementina proposed to leave the estate to her cousin, Sir Paul Benthall KBE, FLS, son of the Rev. Charles Benthall and grandson of Edward the Bengal judge. Sir Paul persuaded her to leave it to the National Trust together with some of its more important contents and part of the necessary endowment. Sir Paul's elder brother, Sir Edward Benthall KCSI (1893–1961), also provided part of the endowment required to maintain the house. When repairs were undertaken in about 1960, it was found that the timbers of the main building were badly damaged by deathwatch beetle, making the restoration of the house a difficult and expensive operation. Further help was provided by Sir Paul and other members of the family, as well as the Historic Buildings Council. The repairs took more than five years to complete.

Mary Clementina Benthall died in 1960 and Sir Edward in 1961. Sir Paul and Lady Benthall then became the first tenants of the National Trust from 1962 to 1985. Sir Paul Benthall had a distinguished career in India. In 1923, he joined Bird & Co., owned by Lord Cable until his death in 1927. The ownership of the company then passed to his son-in-law Edward Benthall. From 1945 Sir Paul became senior partner until his retirement in 1952, when he returned to Britain. During his career in India Sir Paul served two arduous periods during the early years after independence, as President of the Bengal Chamber of Commerce and the Associated Chambers of Commerce which represented all British firms in India, as well as a number of Indian companies in their dealings with the Indian and States governments.

Portrait of the Rev. Charles Benthall on holiday in Morocco, c. 1925, by Alethea Garstin (Great Chamber)

*Portrait of
Sir Paul and
Lady Benthall,
by Richard
Forster, 1984*

As the senior representative of British business interests, he had many meetings with leading Indian politicians including Mohandas 'Mahatma' Gandhi, Jawaharlal Nehru and Chakravarti Rajagopalachariar. After the assassination of Gandhi, he was the only European trustee of the Ghandi Memorial Trust. In recognition of these services he was made a Knight Commander of the British Empire (KBE).

He had also found time to write a serious botanical book on the trees of Calcutta and its neighbourhood, as a result of which he was elected a Fellow of the Linnaean Society. Sir Paul and Lady Benthall were largely responsible for the present appearance of the interior of the house, providing much of the important furniture, books and pictures. Some items were their own; some were acquired when Lindridge, the Devon home of Sir Edward and Lady Ruth Benthall, was sold after the death of Sir Edward in 1961; some came from other members of the family who wished their heirlooms to come to the family home; and some items were bought in order to furnish the rooms open to visitors. Their intention was to keep the feeling and warmth

of a family home while maintaining harmony with the house and its past. Most of the better antique furniture, as well as the family portraits, were bequeathed to the National Trust when they died.

Sir Paul and Lady Benthall's second son James and his wife Jill took on the tenancy in 1985, which enabled Sir Paul and Lady Benthall to continue living in the house until their deaths in 1992 and 1988 respectively.

James and Jill's daughter Katherine, and Rebecca, the daughter of James's twin Richard, were both married in Benthall church in 1990. After Sir Paul's death, James and his three brothers decided to give to the National Trust their parents' collection of Caughley china, the family miniatures and a few other items, so as to leave the home their parents had created as complete as possible.

In 1996 Richard Benthall and his wife Stella took on the tenancy and lived at Benthall until 2004, when they moved to Lindridge. The tenancy has passed to Richard's son Edward and his wife Sally.

BIBLIOGRAPHY

Farrow, W.J., *The Great Civil War in Shropshire*, 1926.

The Garrisons of Shropshire during the Civil War, 1642–48, 1867.

Hall, S.C., FSA, *The Baronial Halls and Ancient Picturesque Edificies of England*, i, 1858.

Harleian Society xxviii, *The Visitation of Shropshire 1623*, p.92.

Avray Tipping, H., *English Homes Period III*, i, 1929.

Cook, Olive, *The English House through Seven Centuries*, 1968.

Transactions of the Shropshire Archaeological Society, xxxv, 1912, p.233.

Benthall church

THE BENTHALL FAMILY

Showing only family members with
a connection to Benthall Hall

Anfrid de Benetala (d. after 1128)
|
Hamon de Benthall
|
Robert de Benthall (d. *c.*1204)
|
Robert de Benthall (d. by 1249)
|
Philip de Benthall (d. *c.*1281)
|
Margery de Benthall = John Burnell de Benthall   Henry de Benthall (d. 1317)
                                                   Abbot of Buildwas
|
Philip de Benthall (active 1330)
|
John de Benthall
|
Walter de Benthall = Anne Cresset
lord in 1363
|
John de Benthall = Cecily Wolrich
(d. after 1407)
|
Walter Benthall = Joan Yonge
|
John Benthall = Agnes Corbett
|
Edmund Benthall = Margery Leighton
|
Robert Benthall = Katherine Wollaston
(active 1521)
|
William Benthall = Agnes Caswall
(d. 1572)
|
Richard Benthall = Iane Ludlowe   Iohn Bentall = Agnes Barbar

                                              (Essex Branch)